# The
# MIRACLE
# That Made Us
# USA

## A "UNITED" NATION

## Betty Lou Rogers

WITH GOD, ALL THINGS ARE POSSIBLE

USA USA

# PROLOGUE

*Somewhere along the way, it seems that social responsibility, in our country, has been very neglected or possibly forgotten! Or it could be some have never heard of this commitment every citizen of our great nation has, to insure the freedoms which were so grimly fought for, and remain for us to enjoy today! Americans, all, should be filled to over-flowing with gratitude, brotherhood, and thankfulness for our wonderful country, created for us by God, and paid for, with the blood, tears, and lives of our brave ancestors! What a beautiful place to live and have fun, work as hard as we want, and have the ability to enjoy a world of spectacular pleasures.*

*These social charges and duties and necessities were handed down to us more than 200 years ago. Our accountability as Americans, have been clearly defined in the documents prepared by our fore-fathers. The Pilgrims were the first to establish our beliefs and goals! Our Declaration of Independence and our Constitution. reiterate those same goals and beliefs, so vital to a good life! They show concern for the human being and his right to survival and self-fulfillment! Human needs do not change. We all want comfort, respect, with a chance to have creative achievement a possibility. There is no denying the fact, that learning to respect all people and wanting to be good citizens is the way that leads toward peaceful and productive lives!*

A strong nation is sensitive to other's needs and wants. A caring nation realizes that courtesy, fair play, and honesty, play a major role in realizing life's goals. And, of course, a wise nation needs smart and tender-hearted people who have a strong desire for learning, and will govern honestly, wisely, and well! The lack of courtesy and respect for our fellow travelers, can be the downfall of a free nation! Being fair-minded and just comes from God, and reinforces the ideals of a free nation. Dishonesty, jealousy, and breaking laws prevent many good things from happening. All these are social responsibilities to manage and own! These behaviors are as necessary to our personal health, as they are to the productive health and well-being of our country! Respect for our family, work, learning, and respect for our fellow Americans, ourselves, and our country, is every citizen's duty and obligation! We are social creatures, and don't live alone. What good times we have socializing! We play ball, not deceit! And respect is the name of the game. Respect others as you respect yourself. Treat them as you like to be treated! No day should pass by without paying tribute to and appreciation for what we really have as blessed and privileged Americans!

# The Miracle That Made Us A "United" Nation!

*For over one hundred years, we were colonies belonging to England, and ruled in later years by King George III. This was a good deal, for the English, because they sold all the needed supplies to these colonies, who were very dependent on provisions coming from England. They were involved in many wars and needed the income. Increasing the taxes on the supplies, going to the colonies, would bring in more revenue. They kept adding taxes, and when they included paper, glass, and tea, it became a big issue in the colonies. The colonies were feeling, that the English were taking advantage of them with these new taxes , and they had no power to control it. "Taxation without representation", became the colonists cry! They began to rebel against English rule.*

1

A group gathered in Boston, boarded an English ship, and dumped English goods, that hadn't been unloaded yet, into Boston Harbor! A lot of tea went overboard, so this event became known as the Boston Tea Party

John Hancock gained fame as a patriot when his ship, Liberty, landed in Boston Harbor with a cargo of Madeira Wine. The crew locked the British customs officer in a cabin, while they unloaded the wine, without paying taxes, to the British. The British seized his ship, but were unsuccessful in trying to get the taxes on the wine! Because of this action, Hancock became popular in the colonies, and the British regarded him as a real threat! He was the first to sign the Declaration of Independence. Even today, when a man signs a document, they say, "put your John Hancock" on it!

*Riots followed, with more rebellion, until the colonists finally decided they wanted to be free of their English rulers, and govern themselves. So, Thomas Jefferson constructed a statement, to the English rulers, informing them the American colonies desired to be free of their taxes and rules!*

*They wanted to be free and independent of England. They wanted a change in government from a government who didn't want to change. This document is called The Declaration of Independence! One of the signers of this document was Benjamin Franklin. He was a very wise, smart man. He saw what was needed to make this decision work. He saw that the colonies had to band together, and work as one, to be strong and successful! He made this famous statement, "We must all hang together, or we shall surely hang separately"!*

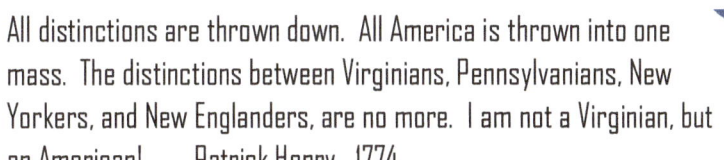

All distinctions are thrown down. All America is thrown into one mass. The distinctions between Virginians, Pennsylvanians, New Yorkers, and New Englanders, are no more. I am not a Virginian, but an American!    Patrick Henry 1774

3

The war, that began because of this rebellion against the English rules, was called, The Revolutionary War. Our thirteen colonies were rebelling and revolting against the English. To win their freedom, they were going to have to fight the British, who had a well-trained army, and a fleet of ships, which would bring over well-trained fighters. The colonies had no army, navy, or experienced soldiers. Most of the men were farmers, and never trained as soldiers! What hurt even more was that all of their supplies, coming from England, had been stopped! And now the American harbors and ports held over a hundred English ships full of soldiers, who were ready to fight!

At the beginning of the war, someone said the American colonies were like a monster with thirteen heads, each one having its own ideas and rules.

4

The war years were difficult and long. George Washington had to form a volunteer army of young untrained men. He had no money, or supplies, like a leader needs. The winters were cold and deadly. At Valley Forge it has been noted that Washington's army suffered from a lack of boots showing many bloody footprints in the snow. And this was only one, of his many problems. Many of this rag-tag army weren't paid on time. They worried about their farms and families back home. Washington was like a father to his troops for he treated his soldiers like sons that he never had. Washington needed support, and the colonies all needed to help. Wise men knew that rules were needed to make all the colonies work together and support the war. We are very remiss and wrong when we dishonor these brave souls who fought for the establishment of our free country. They gave their energy, efforts, and time, sometimes their lives to insure the liberties we enjoy today!

Those who labor in the earth are the chosen people of God, if ever he had a chosen people, whose breasts he has made his peculiar deposit for substantial and genuine virtue!　　　　Thomas Jefferson

5

*A set of rules were written, in the middle of the Revolution, called The Articles of Confederation. But that didn't help because there was no way to enforce the rules. Each state was still acting for itself. The states where the war was taking place, suffered greatly, and paid the biggest price. There was poor communication, so, the other states, who were not close, to the war, didn't know how badly, at times, the war was going. Some didn't help like they should have. Washington needed bullets, food, and clothing for his troops. They needed all the states to pay their fair share, and support this war. Washington, again and again begged for supplies that were always short in coming. But despite all the hurdles these young colonies had, and even with over-whelming odds against them, losing many battles, being without the training or supplies needed, but never giving up, the war was won. Perhaps the passion associated with fighting for ones homeland, with fervor, favored our brave men. The surrender*

at `Yorktown had a very unusual occurrence. Usually, the top officer of each side of the conflict, would meet at a surrender site. The top general of the English army did not show up for the signing, but sent an aide instead. This was like a slap in the face to the colonies, so Washington didn't go, but also sent an aide. The English band played the song, The World Turned Upside Down.

After the war, living in the colonies was very hard, because each state had their own rules, their own money, which wasn't any good in other states. They had stopped paying taxes to the English and didn't want any more taxes! But a government needs money to do its work for the people. But now, with the war ended, there were more problems, than ever! Under English rule, the English had built many forts, out in the west, and the English refused to leave them. The English said, "Make us". Not having an Army, the colonies

were helpless. And not having a Navy, the pirates were capturing Americans, on their ships, and making them slaves. The states couldn't agree on how to handle the Indian problem. Pioneers were coming to this new land and wanted land that belonged to the Native Americans. Most people were poor and in debt. Then, people were thrown into jail if they couldn't pay their debts. The states were all struggling on their own.

Many people were farmers and were struggling to keep their farms, and get help with their debts. Soon many farmers found themselves in jail, because of their debts. A group of farmers revolted against the state of Massachusetts because there was no aid for them. They needed support from their government, which wasn't able to help! This group was called Shay's Rebellion.

8

This group of farmers were defeated, four people were killed, the others fled into the woods. This incident, really scared the people in the colonies! They were on their own with no one to help! The states were all struggling on their own. No citizens were being helped or kept safe. The thirteen heads of the monster were still thinking selfishly, not group-minded at all. Weakness and having no direction, for the colonies, was taking its toll! General Washington was mortified and thought our enemies probably felt triumphant because the colonies were having so much trouble living together. Thomas Jefferson thought a little rebellion kept everyone honest. "The spirit of resistance to government is so valuable, on occasion, that I wish it to be always kept alive,"

Our Founding Fathers. learning the hard way, had found that a weak government was incapable of governing. They also saw that our liberty was also in danger, since they had no way of protecting the rights that liberty inferred! After all, that was the main reason most people had come to this new land. But more and more people were beginning to see there is strength in numbers, so to be strong, the states had to band together, under one set of laws, with a common money system, and a common purpose! They needed a strong nation to deal with other governments. They needed an army and navy to keep everyone safe, in case there was another war. They needed some way to settle differences between the states. Maryland and Virginia were fighting over whose ships had the right to go up and down the Potomac River for they both

*had boundaries on the Potomac. September 1786, a meeting was called for all the states to send someone to Annapolis, Maryland to look for answers to their problems. Only five of the thirteen states sent delegates, so there was very little they could do. All the states had to cooperate in settling the problems. Alexander Hamilton and James Madison wouldn't give up and called for another conference to be held in Philadelphia, Pennsylvania in May 1787. They didn't know exactly what they were going to do, but were hoping to find answers to their common problems. James Madison had the bright idea to, again, use the quarrel between Virginia and Maryland as an excuse to bring the states together. They had to develop a plan for their country! Talking together, they might find a way to settle their problems. They really didn't know they were going to write our Constitution. But they began their discussions, and in talking, they discovered all the*

If a nation expects to be ignorant and free in a state of civilization, it expects what never was and never will be! Thomas Jefferson

11

problems that needed answers. And this is the way to make progress in a group. But they had to be of like minds and desires and have a wish for fairness for all, which at that time was unknown. This group of patriots, dedicated to the common purpose of joining together into a free nation, wrote the rules which guide our nation to this day. The writing and acceptance of our Constitution, a few months later, became, as Washington put it, "a little short of a miracle". Our country kicked and screamed its way into becoming a united country. Like giving birth, the labor was long and hard, lasting a good three and a half long, hot, sweaty months. This convention called for May 14, 1787 asked that all states send a person or persons to Philadelphia to work out a way for our states to agree to work and live safely together.

At the time, Philadelphia was chosen because it was the largest city in America. These persistent souls didn't know

London though handsomer than Paris, is not so handsome as Philadelphia!    Thomas Jefferson

12

they were going to write a constitution, so, they called their meeting the "Grand Convention".

When the Convention opened nothing happened! It had been the rainiest spring in history, and all the roads were mud. Hardly anyone showed up on time. For a while, it looked as though there would never be a convention!

James Madison was the first one there. He had spent a whole year, reading everything he could about government. He had a Plan. He was hoping everyone would like his plan over others which might be presented. It wasn't until the 25th of May, that enough delegates had arrived to begin. George Washington and Ben Franklin, the oldest at 81, had met earlier to discuss the problems they were facing, and to share a good bottle of port. Franklin was sick and didn't think he could attend, but he knew he was needed. So, he arrived, at

Liberty is always dangerous, but it is the safest thing we have! Harry Emerson Fosdick

13

the Convention, in a sedan chair, first ever seen in our country. It was a chair sitting on two long poles, with two convicts at the front, and two convicts at the back carrying the poles. He hired the convicts from the jail that was across the street from the Pennsylvania State House where the convention was held. This was the same place Thomas Jefferson first read his Declaration of Independence to many of the same people. This is why people began to call this building Independence Hall.

George Washington was the most famous delegate. Ben Franklin, James Madison, and Alexander Hamilton were some of the wisest there! Some people, at the Convention, said Hamilton was too smart for his own good! Hamilton was a small young man and good looking. Sometimes, men in those days, who had skinny legs, would put bags of sand in their

I agree with you that there is a natural aristocracy among men. The grounds of this are virtue and talents! Thomas Jefferson

14

stockings to look like muscles. Hamilton never had need of sandbags. People said he had a "graceful turn of the leg".

Women would giggle when some of the bags leaked sand, showing there were no muscles in their skinny legs.

James Madison was a wealthy young man who loved to read. He was very dedicated to serving his country, and his wealth wasn't held against him. He was a short man, "No bigger than a half piece of soap," someone had called him.

People loved and respected Washington. When he had arrived there earlier, people had cheered and cheered as he rode down the street. He was a proud, strong, and energetic fifty-five year old. He was just as God had made him! He was prickly with a quick temper and could bellow like a bull! He was

15

fearless, riding his horses at top speed, and could dance for three hours at a time. He had false teeth that were a poor fit, making clear talking difficult. But he was a good listener and a wonderful leader. It's no wonder he was chosen unanimously as chairman of the Convention.

There were two sides at the Convention. Madison, Franklin, Washington, and Hamilton were "nationalists". They wanted the states to become a strong united nation. Other people feared they would lose some of the freedom they had won by defeating England's rule. They wanted the states able to keep their rights. So, they were called the "states rights" group.

James Madison took on the important job of making notes on what was said each day. He had chosen a seat at the front, so he could hear every word. At the end of each day, he

16

would return to his room and carefully write down the proceedings of the day, using the notes he had made. Sometimes he had twenty pages, for the day, carefully written, all with a quill pen. Madison has been called the father of the Constitution.

The group gathered there, first decided on two strict rules. 1.Everything said each day was a secret. This meant people could speak their minds, with nothing they said, held against them. 2. The delegates were allowed to change their minds. This meant that after hearing more information on a subject, they could change their vote! Listening and learning and being willing to change, is most important, when problem-solving is a must! They proceeded to decide how decisions would be made for their new united states. Madison's plan, called the Virginia Plan, stated that the larger states would have more

votes than the smaller states, because they had more people living there. But the smaller states weren't dumb. If the larger states had more votes, they could rule the smaller states. They wanted equality! But the delegates were fair-minded.

The delegates agreed and disagreed. The smaller states feared the power and influence the larger states could potentially have . They thought the larger states could take over and dominate and neglect considering the will of the majority of the people! The southern states had serious differences with the northern states. Both sides had their own ideas, and ways of living. An answer had to be found! A committee met and found they had to compromise, so they could all agree. This meant that each side would give in a little. This way each side would win some and lose some. They settled on having two

Houses of government. The one House would have votes according to their population. The other House would have two votes per state, giving small states equal power with the larger states. This would be the Upper House, called the Senate. Our House of Representatives are elected every two years. Our Senators are elected for six-year terms.

The delegates had many more problems to solve, and they ended up agreeing more than disagreeing. Their greatest challenge was to set up a government with enough power to act, but government that didn't have too much power. They didn't want one person or group to have the ability to make up laws, on their own, for everyone else. The problem then became, who would stop the House and Senate from voting foolish laws. They needed someone to "check" on the House and Senate. Someone was needed for this job. An elected man, a President, could watch over the House and Senate and keep

The Constitution in all it's provisions, looks to an indestructible Union composed of indestructible States! Salmon Portland Chase

19

them fair, A president could be responsible for this job. The House and Senate can make laws, the president can't, but he can suggest laws. So, the president's position was decided on. No one wanted to have a king, including Washington, who later became the first president. of this infant nation. The president would be elected every four years. And in a democracy, the person chosen by the people is accepted and confirmed as the country's chosen leader! If he doesn't do a good job, four years later, a new leader can be elected. But he should receive the help of all citizens! All patriots, at this time, will think of the good of our country and work toward making and keeping our country prosperous, and safe, with liberty and justice for all!

The delegates knew that a court would be needed to settle disputes between the states. So they set up a Judicial Branch, and ended up with three branches of government, each

20

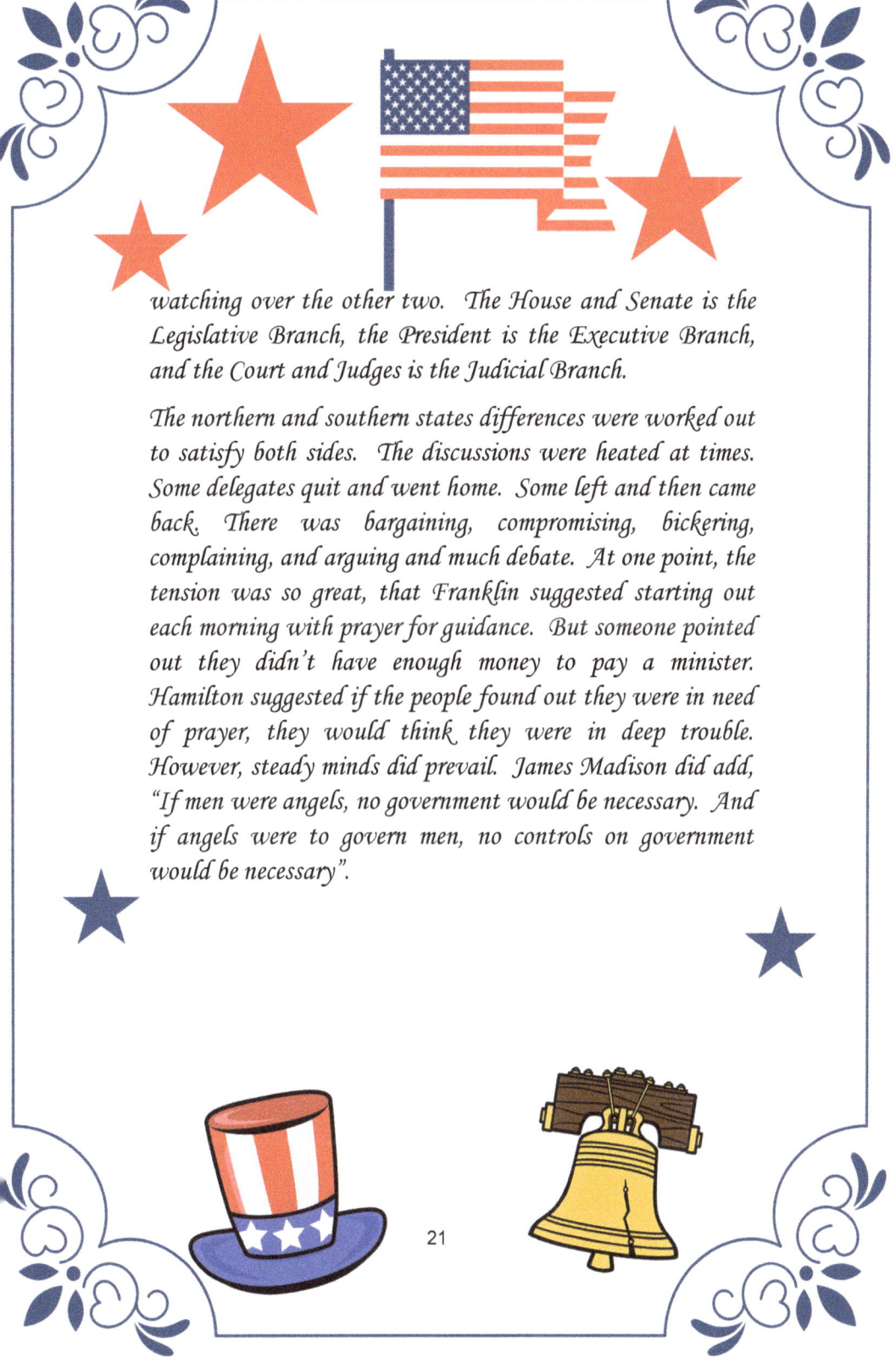

watching over the other two. The House and Senate is the Legislative Branch, the President is the Executive Branch, and the Court and Judges is the Judicial Branch.

The northern and southern states differences were worked out to satisfy both sides. The discussions were heated at times. Some delegates quit and went home. Some left and then came back. There was bargaining, compromising, bickering, complaining, and arguing and much debate. At one point, the tension was so great, that Franklin suggested starting out each morning with prayer for guidance. But someone pointed out they didn't have enough money to pay a minister. Hamilton suggested if the people found out they were in need of prayer, they would think they were in deep trouble. However, steady minds did prevail. James Madison did add, "If men were angels, no government would be necessary. And if angels were to govern men, no controls on government would be necessary".

21

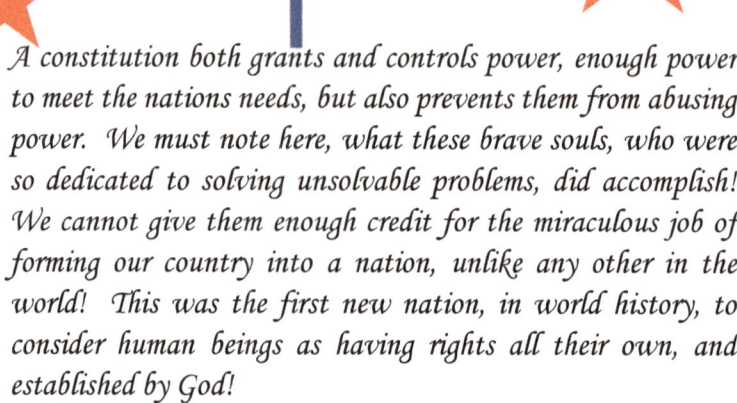

A constitution both grants and controls power, enough power to meet the nations needs, but also prevents them from abusing power. We must note here, what these brave souls, who were so dedicated to solving unsolvable problems, did accomplish! We cannot give them enough credit for the miraculous job of forming our country into a nation, unlike any other in the world! This was the first new nation, in world history, to consider human beings as having rights all their own, and established by God!

By September of that same year, everyone was tired, hot, weary, and ready to go home. They had worked for nearly four months. But they had to sign this document which they all had just written. A committee met and fashioned "the Plan" into a well-written document, for all to read and see the results of all the hard work! On September 17, it was ready for the delegates to sign. The baby was born! They had

No man is above the law, and no man is below it; nor do we ask any man's permission when we require him to obey it!
Theodore Roosevelt

*completed a set of rules that would serve all the states and bind them into a new nation, all for one, and one for all!  It was called our Constitution. They had endured a long, hot summer.  They had even nailed the windows shut because of their secrecy rule.  So, they had no relief from any cooling breezes that open windows might have provided.  But after all the delegates had signed it, the states each had to approve it yet.*

*Ben Franklin had a speech read to the delegation.  One part said, "Many times in my life, I have been absolutely sure I was right, only to change my mind a year or two later.  Some people never change their minds.  They are always rather ridiculous."*

*The newspapers published this written document, so every citizen could see what kind of government had been proposed there in Philadelphia.  Nearly four months from its inception,*

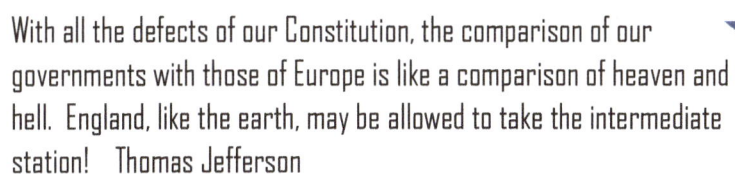

With all the defects of our Constitution, the comparison of our governments with those of Europe is like a comparison of heaven and hell.  England, like the earth, may be allowed to take the intermediate station!   Thomas Jefferson

23

thirty-nine delegates signed The Constitution, and it was on its way to becoming the Supreme Law of the land. Fifty-five delegates started in May, and by September enough had signed it to make it official. Now each state had to decide to join this union by ratifying this Constitution. On December 7, Delaware was the first state to sign. The last state joined in May 1790 . There was one common complaint. It did not contain a Bill of Rights. Each state had made up their own rights of the people, but were wanted to be stated in our Constitution!

After the rule of King George III, this was very important to people everywhere. The first idea of people having rights goes way back in English history to 1215. Many people had been sorely treated and oppressed by their cruel ruler, King John. The English lords made King John sign the Magna Carta. This charter listed the rights that land-owners and church leaders demanded from King John. One of our stated rights is

freedom of religion. Under English rule, many colonists couldn't worship as they pleased. The Church of England was the accepted religion. Baptists and Methodists were often thrown into jail. The rights that we have, declares all persons are free and equal. It also forbids cruel and unusual punishment!

The first of July, 1788, a year after the writing of our Constitution. enough states had approved it for our nation to begin. Our Founding Fathers were wise and humble men, trying to satisfy the needs of our new country. But these bold and brave patriots had one more job to fulfill. They had promised the people that their rights to live in this new nation would be stated in the Constitution. Any additions or changes are called amendments.

So, in 1791 the first ten additions were made to our Constitution, stating the rights of the citizens, of our great nation. These first ten amendments to our Constitution are called the Bill of Rights. Actually the first eight amendments are known as the Bill of Rights, and is addressed to the national government. So the Bill Of Rights states limits of the national but not the state government! They set forth the idea that a free society is freedom of conscience and freedom of expression. Freedom of religion, speech, press, assembling, bearing arms, is part of our basic charter of liberties that are listed! George Washington and James Madison called all this work they had accomplished, a "miracle"! Was it because it was done in less than four months, or that it still works today? Or is it a miracle that answers were found and put

I do believe we shall continue to grow, to multiply and prosper until we exhibit an association, powerful, wise, and happy, beyond what has yet seen by man! Thomas Jefferson

into action by patriots, who had so much respect for the needs of their people? They were able to put their differences aside, think of others, and do what was needed to meet their goal. And, they did what was right! Do we have this kind of people working for us today? Working selfishly, unbiased, willing to look at the whole picture, willing to change ones perspective, and putting aside grudges is the way to success!

Our Constitution begins with a statement disclosing what the writers were trying to accomplish. This preamble tells us that we Americans want to work together. We want everyone to get a fair deal. We want to get along with each other. We want to defend ourselves. We want our country to run smoothly. We want liberty for our families, and ourselves!

As the Constitution won the support of Americans, it became a symbol of a Golden Age. It became a part of the American

creed. It stood for liberty, equality before the law, and limited government. Our Constitution both grants and controls power. Enough power to meet the nations needs, but also prevents them from abusing power. We must recognize the creative feat these framers accomplished! After all, we are the only country in the world, who has a birthdate to celebrate!

Freedom is the one single word that summarizes the purpose and the meaning of America. The Pilgrims were the first to take part in the greatest adventure ever, when they sought freedom to pursue their own religion. When the American colonists demanded their freedom from English rule to govern themselves, we must note and acknowledge this act was the greatest political experiment in history!

The real strength of America, is not that America has completely achieved ideal freedom, but as a country, we see

28

and never stop trying to perfect that dream, and reaching that ideal! We should always keep trying to be better! Everyone should want to make lives better. If something is wrong, or unfair, do something about it! But do it the American way! Lawfully and urgently pursue the problem! That way, we honor our forefathers who wanted our country to serve each and every citizen!

Our forefathers, who founded our great nation, devoted their life's work to the legacy of liberty. Our freedoms did not come about by accident! They were paid for with the blood of our ancestors. All of us enjoy those freedoms, as we grow up and live in a land where human rights, and God-given freedom of the individual are respected! Our legacy of liberty is our greatest legacy, settled for and provided, to us, by our ancestors!

*They also saw the necessity of being able to control and change their government?  We, like these brave souls, should be brave and bold to uphold our laws, abide by them, and keep our nation strong, honest, and true!  We must be patriots like our Founding Fathers!  We can carry on the work of our ancestors by honoring those people who act as stewards of the laws of our land.   They are dedicated to serving our population, by responding to every  person's care and needs, protect us from those people who do not appreciate our great country by respecting the laws of our land, and all the privileges which are ours, and which are not available in any other country in the world!*

*Our Constitution was written in 1787.  It has lasted over 230 years, longer than any other written constitution. Thomas*

Of all human powers operating on the affairs of mankind, none is greater than that of competition!   Henry Clay

30

Jefferson called the new Constitution, "unquestionably, the wisest ever yet presented to men."

The first of July, 1788, a year after the writing of our Constitution, enough states had approved it for our nation to be underway with our new, nationally approved set of rules. That was a very special and exciting Fourth of July celebration, our birthdate, remembering and noting our independence. This celebration in Philadelphia that was held, equaled no other. A ship in the harbor, boomed its cannons as five thousand paraders got ready to march. Everything and everyone was celebrated in the parade held that day. The parade lasted from eight in the morning, until six in the evening.

Leading the parade, was a herald with a trumpet, proclaiming the New Age! Riders on horseback, carried banners celebrating everything worth celebrating. A float with an enormous framed Constitution was a hit. Four hundred fifty

architects and carpenters marched in the procession. High-stepping bands, sawmakers, farmers with four-ox plows, weavers, brickmakers, boat builders, bakers, corsetmakers preachers, and many, many more, proudly displayed their pleasure at what the Framers had accomplished. It was just short of a miracle! And the day ended with a picnic spread out for seventeen thousand people!

John Adams, who became our second president following George Washington had this to say, as a prediction and counsel. The second day of July, 1776, will be the most memorable epoch in the history of America! I am apt to believe that it will be celebrated by succeeding generations as the great anniversary festival. It ought to be commemorated as the day of deliverance, by solemn acts of devotion to God Almighty. Our country was founded on basic Christian beliefs! We are under God's care and trust!

### Foreign Aid to the Colonies

*England had foes and rivals in Europe, and they began to take a cautious attitude toward this rebellion against England. Adventurers flocked to America, hoping to make fortunes and win glory for themselves, but Washington discounted most of them as disappointments. A Prussian officer helped train Washington's army. Lafayette, belonging to French nobility, was given a major general's commission by Washington, which was an excellent political investment.*

*The French and Spanish sent valuable supplies and loaned money to the rebellious colonies. Benjamin Franklin went to France, seeking further aid. Both France and Spain went to war with England, but, were less interested in helping the colonies and more interested in humbling England. The French did help win Washington's last major battle against Cornwallis at Yorktown, which ended the serious fighting of the war.*

And always remember, never forget - - -

America is your homeland,
'Twas won with blood and strife,
And cherish all your freedoms,
And guard them with your life!

34

# The "Miracle" That Made Us A "United" Nation!

*Betty Lou Rogers*

*The order of states signing our Constitution*

1. Delaware 1787
2. Pennsylvania 1787
3. New Jersey 1787
4. Georgia 1788
5. Connecticut 1788
6. Massachusetts 1788
7. Maryland 1788
8. South Carolina
9. New Hampshire 1788
10. Virginia 1788
11. New York 1788
12. North Carolina 1789
13. Rhode Island 1790

This is the 13 colonies who birthed our wonderful nation. They are the birth-parents of our liberty and freedoms we enjoy today!

14. Vermont 1791
15. Kentucky 1792
16. Tennessee 1796
17. Ohio 1803

18. Louisiana 1812
19. Indiana 1816
20. Mississippi 1817
21. Illinois 1818
22. Alabama 1819
23. Maine 1820
24. Missouri 1821

25. *Arkansas  1836*
26. *Michigan  1837*
27. *Florida  1845*
28. *Texas  1845*
29. *Iowa  1846*
30. *Wisconsin  1848*
31. *California  1850*
32. *Minnesota 1858*
33. *Oregon  1859*
34. *Kansas  1861*
35. *West Virginia  1863*
36. *Nevada  1864*
37. *Nebraska  1867*
38. *Colorado  1876*
39. *North Dakota  1889*
40. *South Dakota  1889*
41. *Montana  1889*
42. *Washington 1889*
43. *Idaho  1890*
44. *Wyoming  1890*
45. *Utah  1896*
46. *Oklahoma 1907*
47. *New Mexico 1912*
48. *Arizona  1912*
49. *Alaska  1959*
50. *Hawaii  1959*

No man is above the law, and no man is below it;  nor do we ask any man's permission when we require him to obey it!   Theodore Roosevelt

Some Quotable Quotes:

Before the Revolutionary War

*If we are wise, let us prepare for the worst, There is nothing which will so soon produce a speedy and honorable peace as a state of preparation for war; and we must either do this, or lay our account to patch up an inglorious peace, after all the toil, blood, and treasure we have spent!   George Washington*

*Let it be remembered that civil liberty consists not in a right to every man to do just what he pleases; but it consists in an equal right to all the citizens to have, enjoy, and do, in peace, security, and without molestation, what ever the equal and constitutional laws of the country admit to be consistent with the public good! John Jay  1790 Justice in Supreme Court*

*Every man who loves peace, every man who loves his country, every man who loves liberty, ought to have the Constitution ever before his eyes, that he may cherish in his heart a due attachment to the Union of America, and be able to set a due value on the means of preserving it!   James Madison*

*Our cause is the cause of all mankind, and we are fighting for their liberty in defending our own.  It is a glorious task assigned us by Providence, which has I trust, given us spirit and virtue equal to it, and will at last crown it with success!  Benjamin Franklin*

*Franklin Declares War*

*Mr. Strahan, You are a member of Parliament, and one of that majority which has doomed my country to destruction. You have begun to burn our towns and murder our people. Look upon your hands! They are stained with the blood of your relations! You and I were long friends; you are now my enemy, and I am yours, B. Franklin (A letter written in 1775, but not mailed)*

*Thousands of words have been written about our American Revolution, that long and bitter struggle which culminated in the formulation, for the first time in the world's history of a self-governing organization founded on the principle that every individual has an equal right to life, liberty, and the pursuit of happiness. We will never know the temper of the times or the enormous sacrifices made by our forefathers, to make possible the freedoms we now take for granted!*

*I find the great thing in this world is not so much where we stand, as in which direction we are moving: To reach the port of heaven, we must sail sometimes with the wind and sometimes against it -- but we must sail, and not drift, nor lie at anchor!*
*Oliver Wendell Holmes*

*I pledge allegiance to the flag*
*of the United States of America*
*and to the Republic for which it stands,*
*one nation under God, indivisible,*
*with liberty and justice for all.*

*The American's Creed*

*I believe in the United States of America as a*
*Government of the people, by the people, for the people;*
*whose just power are derived from the consent of the*
*governed; a democracy in a republic; a sovereign Nation*
*of many sovereign States; a perfect Union, one and*
*inseparable; established upon the principles of freedom,*
*equality, justice, and humanity for which American*
*patriots sacrificed their lives and fortunes.*

*I therefore believe it is my duty to my country to love*
*it, to support its Constitution; to obey its laws; to*
*respect its flag and to defend it against all enemies.*

*William Tyler Page*